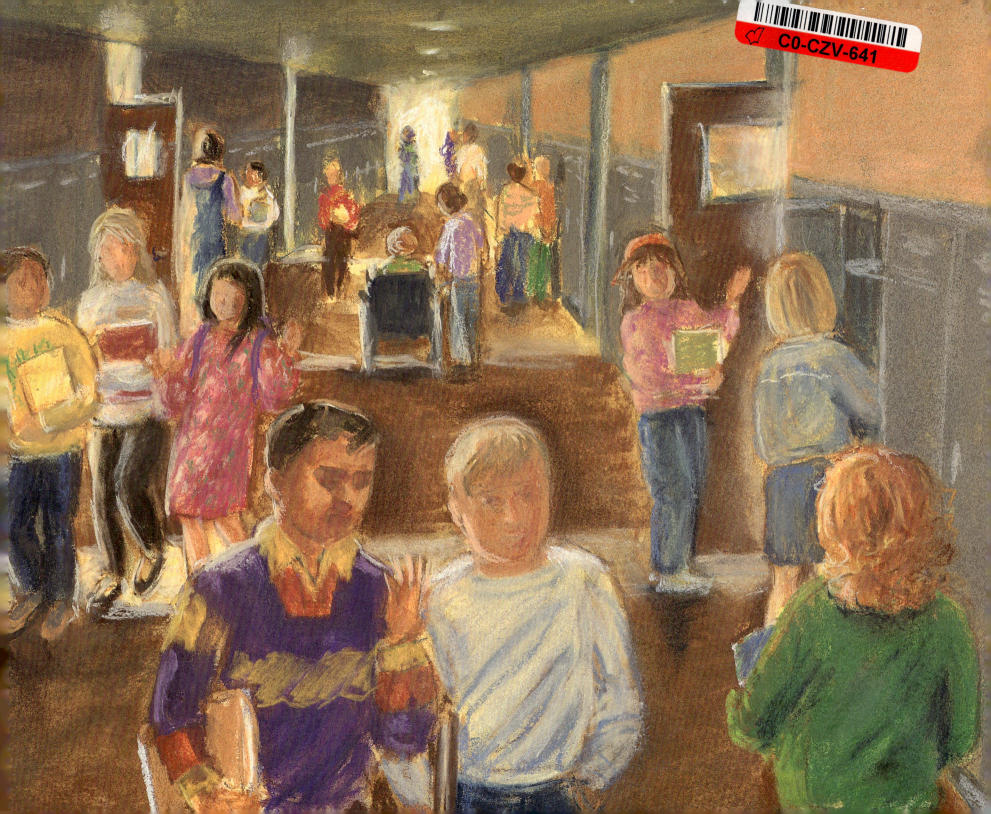

Tilbury House, Publishers
132 Water Street
Gardiner, ME 04345

First edition

Text designed on Crummett Mountain by Edith Allard
Editing and production: Mark Melnicove
Editing and production assistance: Liz Pierson and Devon Phillips
Office: Jolene Collins
Imagesetting: High Resolution, Inc., Camden, Maine
Color Separations: Graphic Color Service, Fairfield, Maine
Printing: The Eusey Press, Leominster, Massachusetts
Binding: Quebecor Printing Book Press, Brattleboro, Vermont

Acknowledgments
Malara Kong
Students and teachers at Farrington School, Augusta, Maine
Students at Rieche School, Portland, Maine
Richard Silliboy
Amari and Carole Carmichael
Christi Rentsch Moraga and Family
Lillian Rourke
Laurel and Jayne Hrabarchuk
Sara Shed and Joel, Eli, Aaron, and Hannah Davis
Elwood Green
Winnie McPhederan
Jim Perkins and Theresa Kerchner
Dianne Webb Payne
Nancy and Richard Kelly
Don Reutershan
Elizabeth Wells
Nancy McGinnis
Barbara Livingston
Sheila Wilensky-Lanford
Val Hart
Grace Valenzuela

Who Belongs Here? An American Story is dedicated to my students and to the ESL–English-as-a-Second-Language–teachers of Maine.
Margy Burns Knight

For my immigrant friends and family.
Anne Sibley O'Brien

Who Belongs Here?
An American Story

Margy Burns Knight

Illustrated by Anne Sibley O'Brien

Tilbury House, Publishers
Gardiner, Maine

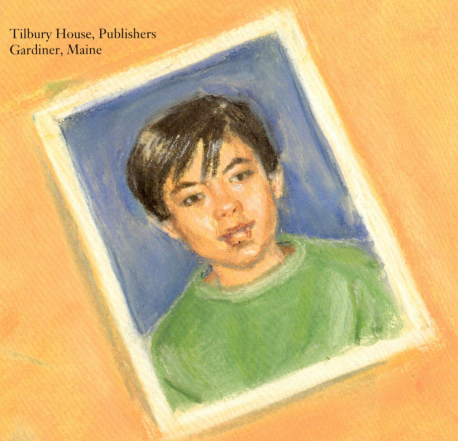

Proceeds from the sale of this book will be given to
educational organizations that teach tolerance.

Mrs. Lenahan's Class

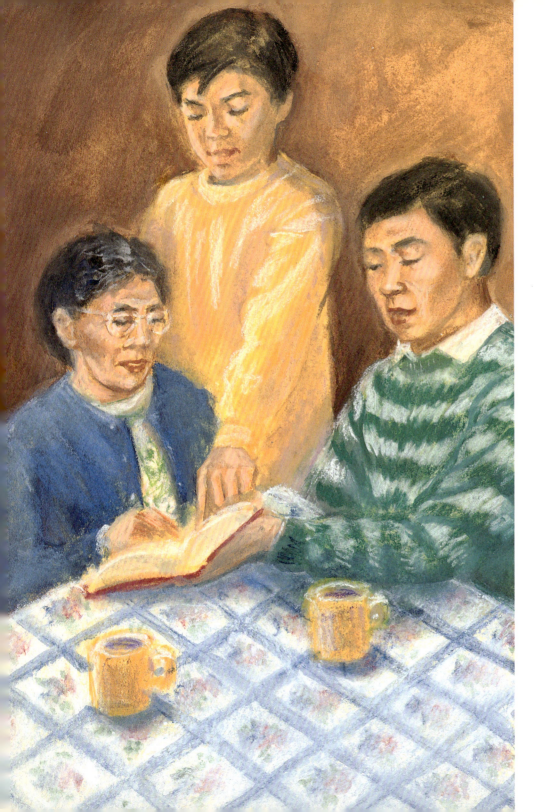

Nary lives with his grandmother and Uncle Savy. He was born in Cambodia and moved to the United States from a refugee camp in Thailand.

Nary left Cambodia because of a civil war. For four years, an army known as the Khmer Rouge led by a man named Pol Pot, separated thousands of Cambodians from their families and forced them to work on farms where they had very little to eat.

Pol Pot told the people he was going to build a stronger Cambodia, but Nary's family and many other families were hungry and scared and hated the guns that killed millions of people–including Nary's parents.

Nary was sad and confused after his parents died. He cried as his grandmother carried him on her back through the jungle to Thailand. He had tried to run, but the blisters on his feet were bleeding. His uncle told him to be quiet because they were running from the soldiers and didn't want to be caught.

In Thailand they lived for several years in a crowded refugee camp where Nary sometimes went to school and his uncle and grandmother helped in the health clinic.

In the last five hundred years millions of people have made the U.S. their home. Some came by choice, while others were forced from their homelands by war, slavery, or famine. For at least 10,000 years before this, the U.S. was inhabited by thousands of tribes of native people. Descendents of these tribes live in the U.S. today.

Nary traveled to the U.S. on a plane. Around his neck he wore a tag with his name, picture, and date of arrival in New York City. Nary was very happy to be moving to the States, but he was nervous because he wasn't sure what was going to happen. Nary's family was met at the airport by their sponsor who helped them settle into their new home.

From 1892 to 1954 more than 12 million immigrants from at least 50 countries arrived on boats at Ellis Island, an immigration station in New York City. Numbered tags were handed to the passengers as they left their ship. Each number matched a number on a big list that officials used as they examined the immigrants for contagious diseases and questioned them about their jobs, money, and destinations. Only 2 out of every 100 people who were examined were not allowed to make the U.S. their new home.

When Nary's family arrived in the U.S. his grandmother was carrying a plastic bag. In it were identity papers, two family photos, and x-rays that showed that her family didn't have active tuberculosis. Nary brought with him his memories of Cambodia and Khmer, the language he learned as a baby. Somedays learning English is frustrating for Nary, but his friends and teachers are helping him. On rainy days he laughs as he tells his grandmother it's raining cats and dogs.

At least 350 languages are spoken in the U.S. today, and many English-language words come from other languages. Kindergarten is a German word that means children's garden, and Mississippi is a Chippewa word for large river. Jeans became the English word for Genés, which is the French spelling of Genoa, a city in Italy. The original material for jeans was imported from Genoa.

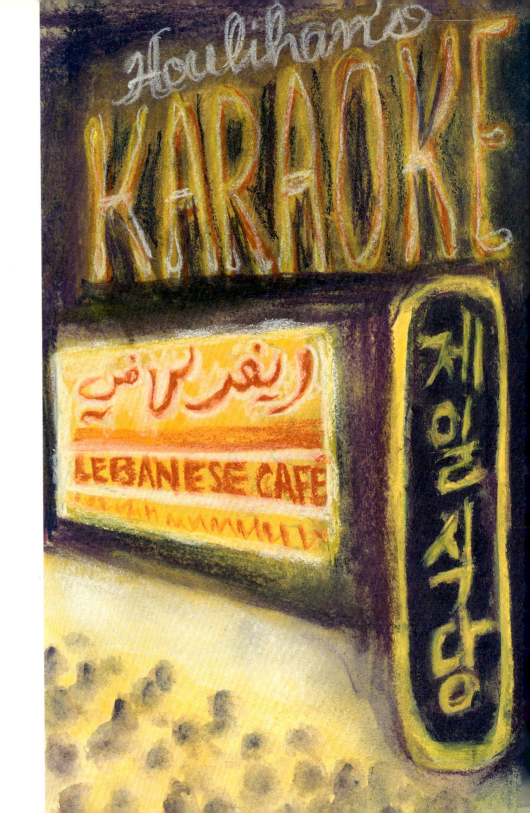

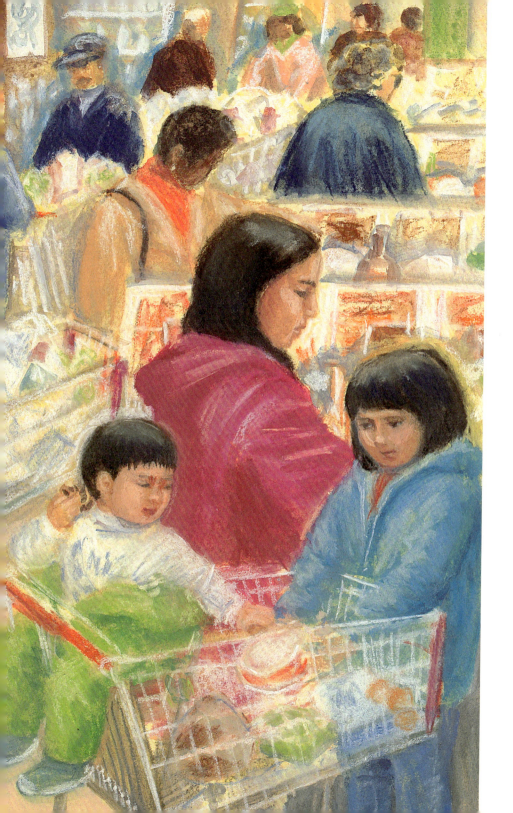

Nary had little to eat during the war in Cambodia. He is amazed by the amount of food in his local grocery store.

His grandmother sends money to Cambodia each month so her relatives can buy seeds to plant rice.

Nary eats rice everyday. Sometimes he eats it with meat or vegetables. He likes it when pizza and ice cream are served at school for lunch.

Peanuts, peppers, corn, squash, and avocados are among America's native foods. Bagels, tortillas, olive oil, curry, potatoes, pretzels, and rice are some of the many foods brought to the U.S. from other countries.

People have been eating rice for over 4,000 years. It originated in Southeast Asia and Spanish explorers brought it to the West Indies at least 500 years ago. Today 8,000 varieties of rice are grown throughout the world. About 15 varieties are grown in the U.S.

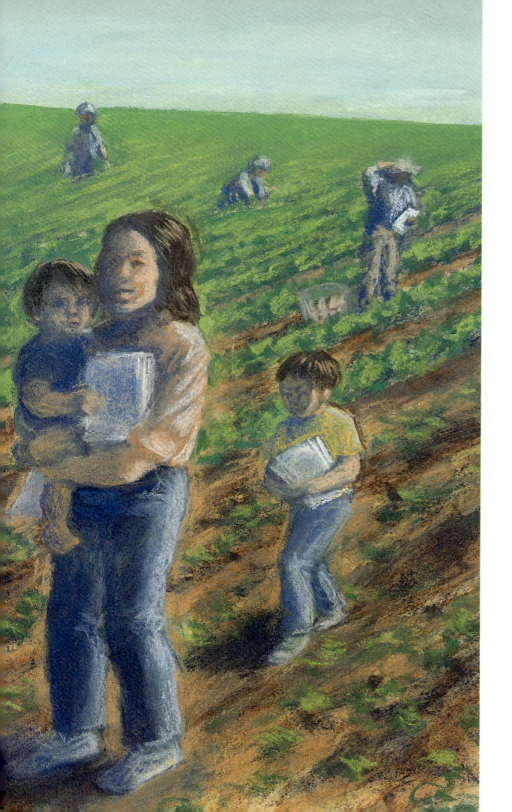

Nary admires Dith Pran because he is working for peace in Cambodia. Like Nary, Dith Pran escaped from the killing fields of Cambodia. Now he travels around the U.S. talking about his hopes for his homeland. It is hard for him to repeat his sad stories, but he wants peace in Cambodia and feels it is important to talk about the terrible things that have happened and continue to happen there.

Dolores Huerta also travels around the U.S. giving talks. For almost 40 years she has helped organize farm laborers. Often, when she'd go to the fields to talk to the workers, she brought her children with her. Many of the people who pick the fruits and vegetables that are sold throughout the U.S. have moved here for better jobs. Dolores Huerta and many others are working with the United Farm Workers of America, so that all farm workers can be healthy, safe, and treated fairly.

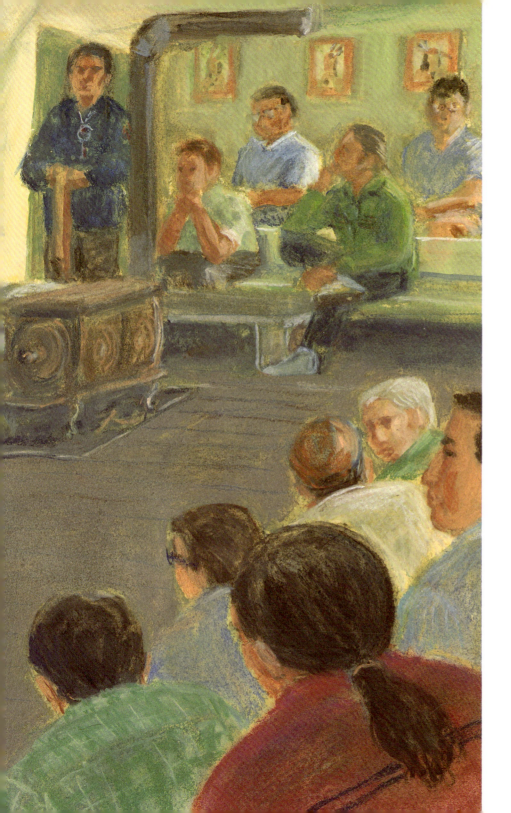

In Nary's new home soldiers don't pound on the door and tell him to get out as they did in Cambodia. Nary likes his new freedom, and at school he is learning about the U.S. Constitution.

Parts of the U.S. Constitution were modeled after the Great Law of Peace, a political system that six nations of Iroquois people developed in the 1500s and used for several hundred years. Representatives of each nation spent long hours talking about ways to build peace and cooperation among their people.

Every year Iroquois people meet at the Six Nations Convention in New York to commemorate the Great Law of Peace.

Nary remembers his grandmother telling him that she had heard the U.S. was going to be better than heaven–full of food and peace. Nary wants to live in peace, so he doesn't understand why some of his classmates are mean to him.

Recently, as he was getting books out of his locker, two classmates said,

"Hey, chink, out of my way."

"Yeah, get back on the boat and go home where you belong."

What if Nary was forced to go back to Cambodia?

What if everyone who now lives in the U.S., but whose ancestors came from another country, was forced to return to his or her homeland?

What if everyone who lives in the U.S. was told to leave?

Who would be left?

Nary can't leave. He has no place to go. The fighting continues in Cambodia and the refugee camps in Thailand are closing.

Who belongs here?

What is a real American?

Every year millions of people from all over the world try to come to the U.S. Not all of them are allowed to live here. Since the mid-1800s the government has made laws to keep certain people out of this country.

Many people choose to come illegally. In Haiti families have built boats so they can leave their island. They hope to find a peaceful, safe home. U.S. Coast Guard ships have been ordered to block these boats from the U.S. shores.

Who should be allowed to come to the U.S.?

Should anyone be made to leave?

If there aren't enough jobs, homes, and food for everyone, how do we decide who gets to live here?

After school Nary went home and talked with his grandmother. He was mad and hurt by his class-mates' words. Last week someone called him a *gook* and told him he didn't belong in the U.S. Nary doesn't want to be afraid to go to school.

Many people who have moved to the U.S. have been treated unkindly. In the 1800s, a potato famine forced thousands of Irish citizens to leave their country. Many Irish immigrants were told not to apply for jobs in the U.S. because they were foreigners and would take away jobs from Americans.
    Has anything like this happened to you or anyone you know?

Nary doesn't like to be called names. He worries that the kids in his school might gang up on him.

Nary has asked the kids who bother him to leave him alone. He'd rather play soccer than fight. Someday he'd like the chance to become a mechanic.

For years many people have worked for change. They are tired of the namecalling, disrespect, hate, and fear, so they protest. Some people walk in marches, others write letters to newspapers or government officials, and some even go to jail for their beliefs. Many people have been involved in boycotts, and others work to get new laws passed.

Do you know anyone who is working for change? Are there changes you would like to help make happen? What can you do?

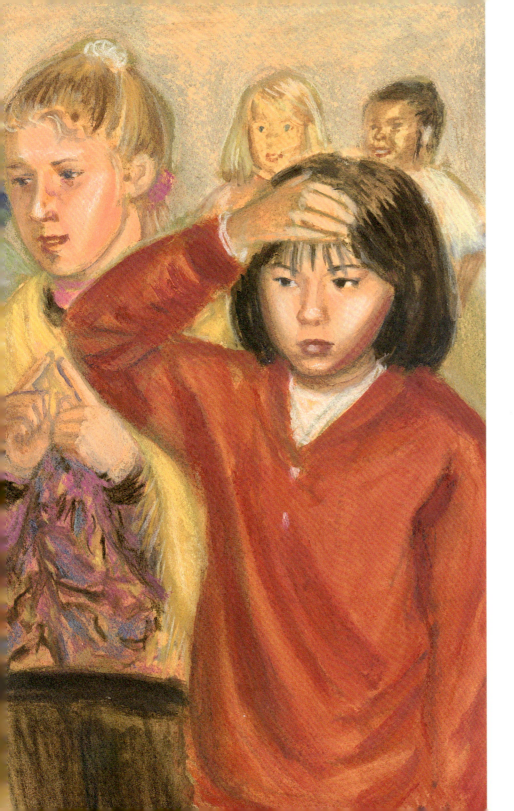

Nary was upset that his classmates didn't understand how it felt to be a refugee. He told his teacher and together they planned a lesson for his social studies class.

Each student pretended to be a refugee. The students had to try to convince non-English-speaking guards that they were refugees seeking asylum. Patting his stomach, one student said, "thúc ăn," the Vietnamese word for *food*. Another student said "dom," as she built the shape of a house with her fingers; her grandmother had taught her the Polish word for *home*.

The lesson reminded Nary of his own experiences and he told his classmates that no one should have to be a refugee. He wished that everyone would have enough food and that all the guns would be taken away.

Many people in Nary's family are still refugees. His family was very surprised to hear that cousin Sokha was getting married because they'd thought Pol Pot's army had killed her. Instead, she had escaped to a refugee camp in Thailand, and now lives in Canada. When Nary returned from her wedding, he put photographs of the celebration in his album.

At school Nary is drawing pictures of the Cambodia he remembers, and he will put those in his album, too.

Each of us has stories to tell about our lives, our memories, and our dreams. Sharing our stories, and listening to each other, help us to understand who we are.

Nary is working hard to make the U.S. his new home. He likes to be with his friends and he is learning to play the drums.

Nary has learned to write Khmer so he can keep in touch with his relatives. He wonders if there will ever be peace in Cambodia. He also hopes people in his new country can learn to get along.

Notes

Who Belongs Here? is based on my experiences as a teacher of ESL—English as a Second Language. My elementary and middle school students often asked me what it meant to be a "chink" or a "gook" and didn't understand why some of their peers told them to go home because they didn't belong in the U.S. Once I asked my students what would happen if everyone who had ancestors who had come to the U.S. were told to leave. Who would be left? Nary's story is a blend of many of my students' lives. I have chosen to write his story as if he were about ten years old, the age of an elementary or middle school student, even though some of my original students are now in their late teens and early twenties.

Pol Pot

Pol Pot's real name is Soloth Sar. Pol Pot is his "nom du guerre," or war name. He grew up in Cambodia and studied politics in France. Pol Pot thought he could make Cambodia stronger by building a farm-based communist society.

During the four years Pol Pot was in power in Cambodia, 1975 to 1979, more than one million people were killed by his army, The Khmer Rouge. Many people died of starvation because they were given almost no food as they labored on farms from dawn to dusk.

Pol Pot no longer lives in Cambodia and is not the official leader of the Khmer Rouge. A United Nations peace-keeping force is now in Cambodia working with the different factions of government, including the Khmer Rouge.

Dith Pran

Dith Pran now lives in New York City where he works as a photojournalist for the *New York Times*. Pol Pot did not want people to be educated, so during his escape from Cambodia Pran pretended he was illiterate in Khmer and French. *The Killing Fields* is a movie about Dith Pran's life during the Pol Pot regime.

Ports of Entry

Today New York and Los Angeles are the main entry points for immigrants arriving to the U.S. People also arrive through the land borders of Mexico and Canada.

Ellis Island opened in 1892 and was one of many immigration stations that have processed immigrants to the U.S. It closed in 1954 and reopened as a museum in 1990.

Angel Island Immigration Station, off the coast of San Francisco, California, may also reopen as a museum. It operated as a detention center for Chinese immigrants from 1910 to 1940. Many immigrants waited for months to be processed by the immigration officials. Some detainees used the walls of the barracks to write poems about their wait. Many of these poems have been published and the walls will be part of the museum.

Refugee

A refugee, according to the United Nations, is a "person who, owing to the well-founded fear of being persecuted for reasons of race, religion, nationality or political opinion, or belonging to a particular social group, is outside the country of his nationality."

There are more than 20 million refugees in the world and 80 percent of them are children and women.

Dolores Huerta

Dolores Huerta is the mother of 11 children. Born in New Mexico, she has lived for many years in California. She tries to help farm workers because she cares for people and wants to make the world better for others. She helps make policies for the United Farm Workers of America and often gives speeches about her work.

Immigration Laws

Immigration laws were not passed in the U.S. until the 1870s. In 1882 the Chinese Exclusion Act banned Chinese workers from entering the country. In the next 35 years laws were written to keep out 33 categories of people, including political radicals and people who could not read and write.

Quotas, rules limiting the number of people allowed to enter the U.S., were established for certain countries in 1924. Many of these quotas kept people from southern and eastern Europe out of the U.S. because some thought these people wouldn't make good citizens.

By the 1960s many people were questioning the fairness of quotas, and the Nationality Act in 1965 changed many of the quotas. In 1980 and 1986, respectively, the Refugee Act and Reform Act were passed to deal with the large numbers of refugees and illegal aliens coming to the U.S.

Repatriation

Repatriation is an effort by the United Nations and other organizations to help groups of refugees, some of whom spend years in refugee camps, return to their country and start a new life. Repatriation is taking place in many countries, including Laos, Cambodia, and El Salvador.

In Cambodia, many returnees were promised land to farm, but much of this land is unsafe because of land mines. Many people who returned to Cambodia from refugee camps in Thailand that closed, were given rice rations, but their food is running out. Even though there are some programs set up to help these people resettle, many are worried that they won't be safe, won't be able to make a living, and that they will be forced to become refugees again.

Iroquois Confederation

Originally, the Iroquois Confederation was composed of five tribes or nations: the Onondaga, Cayuga, Oneida, Mohawk, and Seneca. The Tuscarora joined the league in the early 1700s. Hiawatha, a Mohawk, traveled among the tribes to help to unify them. His hard work resulted in a successful political alliance that held together until the mid-1700s.

Some historians say that the writers of the United States Constitution used the unwritten democratic political organization of the Iroquois Confederation as a model for their writings. Other historians say there is not enough evidence to prove that some of the writers of the Constitution spent time talking to Iroquois leaders about their form of government.

Since the 1840s the Iroquois people have met annually for the Six Nations Convention. The first day of the convention is called the handshaking. Visitors present their wampum, a string of beads or shells.

Some of the meeting takes place in longhouses, the traditional Iroquois homes.

For Further Study

If you who enjoyed this book, you may be interested in the *Who Belongs Here? Activity Guide* by Margy Burns Knight and Thomas V. Chan. It's available for $12.95 postpaid from Tilbury House, Publishers, 132 Water Street, Gardiner, ME 04345.